JUNIOR MARTIAL ARTS
Handling Peer Pressure

Junior Martial Arts

All Around Good Habits
Confidence
Concentration
Hand-Eye Coordination
Handling Peer Pressure
Safety
Self-Defense
Self-Discipline
Self-Esteem

JUNIOR MARTIAL ARTS
Handling Peer Pressure

KIM ETINGOFF

MASON CREST

Mason Crest
450 Parkway Drive, Suite D
Broomall, PA 19008
www.masoncrest.com

Printed and bound in the United States of America.

First printing
9 8 7 6 5 4 3 2 1

Series ISBN: 978-1-4222-2731-2
ISBN: 978-1-4222-2736-7
ebook ISBN: 978-1-4222-9069-9

The Library of Congress has cataloged the
        hardcopy format(s) as follows:

Library of Congress Cataloging-in-Publication Data

Etingoff, Kim.
  Handling peer pressure / Kim Etingoff.
      pages cm. – (Junior martial arts)
   ISBN 978-1-4222-2736-7 (hardcover) – ISBN 978-1-4222-2731-2 (series) – ISBN 978-1-4222-9069-9 (ebook)
 1. Martial arts–Juvenile literature. 2. Peer pressure–Juvenile literature. I. Title.
  GV1101.35.E79 2014
  796.8–dc23
                                    2013004749

Publisher's notes:
The websites mentioned in this book were active at the time of publication. The publisher is not responsible for websites that have changed their addresses or discontinued operation since the date of publication. The publisher will review and update the website addresses each time the book is reprinted.

Contents

MORE THAN FIGHTING

What if you could be stronger? What if you could feel better about who you are? What if you could be better at school?

You can make all of those things happen. You just have to know how. One way to make them happen is to take martial arts!

Martial arts teach you how to defend yourself and fight. They're about getting in shape and moving your body. But that's not the only thing practicing martial arts teaches you. Martial arts are about much more than fighting. They can also teach you how to be a better person.

Learning About Martial Arts

Martial arts aren't anything new. They've been around for a long time. People **practiced** some kinds of martial arts thousands of years ago. Since then, martial arts have changed into the sports we know today.

When we talk about martial arts, we're really talking about a lot of different things. Each kind of martial art is a little different. But they all teach **self-defense**.

You can choose to take classes in all sorts of martial arts. You might have heard of martial arts like karate, judo, and taekwondo. Karate and judo are from Japan. Taekwondo is from Korea.

Keep your eyes open for classes in other kinds of martial arts too. Capoeira is a martial art from Brazil. It has dancing and music. Muay Thai is from Thailand. Aikido comes from Japan. There are many more kinds of martial arts from Asia, Europe, and Latin America.

In today's world, you can take any kind of martial art you want. You don't have to live in Japan to take aikido, for example. Your town might have classes for kinds of martial arts from the other side of the world.

Each martial art is a little bit different. You practice some by yourself and some with a partner. Some are more like sports where people **compete** in fights. A few use fake weapons. There's a martial art out there for you, if you look hard enough.

Spotlight on Muay Thai

Muay thai is a kind of boxing from Thailand. It doesn't use any weapons. You use your hands, feet, elbows, and knees. Students train to be in boxing matches. The point of a match is to win. Muay thai also teaches respect. It teaches self-confidence. It teaches all the things other martial arts teach students who practice them.

HANDLING PEER PRESSURE

Muay Thai fighters wear gloves and pads on their legs. They have to fight in a ring, just like boxing.

Life Skills

All martial arts teach you how to defend yourself from an attack. But martial arts are about way more than just fighting. Martial arts give you new ways of thinking and can help make you a better person.

When you learn how to defend yourself, lots of things happen. Your body gets stronger. You build up muscles. You get better balance. You are more **flexible** and can move in new ways.

As you get better at martial arts, you become more confident too. That means you feel better about what your body can do. You can be proud of how much you've learned in martial arts. You can feel good about who you are and what you can do.

Martial arts can also help you do well in school. You learn how to focus better. Then you'll be able to pay attention to homework, tests, and what the teacher is saying.

You'll learn respect. That means treating others the way you'd like to be treated. You'll respect yourself more. And you'll respect others, like friends, family, and teachers.

No one wants to feel left out! Sometimes, we give in to peer pressure because we want to be part of a group or fit in with others.

That's a lot you can learn from martial arts! But it doesn't all happen at once. You have to work hard at martial arts. It can take time to learn the **skills** that martial arts teach. You'll probably see changes after a few weeks. Even more things will change if you stick with a martial art for months or years!

Peer Pressure

Martial arts are a great way to learn how to fight peer pressure.

"Peer pressure" is made up of two words. "Peer" means someone who is your age and who goes to school with you. All of your classmates are peers. "Pressure" means trying to get someone to do something.

Peer pressure is when your friends or others your age try to get you to make a choice that you wouldn't normally make.

We sometimes talk about peer pressure when it comes to drugs and alcohol. If someone in school is telling you to take drugs or drink alcohol and you don't want to, they're peer pressuring you.

Peer pressure is bad when it makes you do something wrong or against the law. It's peer pressure if someone wants you to skip school. Or to smoke a cigarette.

When you're younger, peer pressure might look a little different. Let's say a group of kids comes up to you and asks you if you want to be mean to another kid on the playground. You don't want to, because you like that person. And you know being mean to other people is wrong.

But they keep peer pressuring you. They tell you it will be fun. They say you have to do it. You don't want to, but you end up saying yes. Then you feel bad because you know you made the wrong decision. But you felt like you didn't have a choice!

Peer pressure can push you to do things that you feel bad about. But sometimes peer pressure can be a good thing. It can help you make good choices. Maybe all your friends play a sport. You're too afraid to try it. But all your friends are doing it, and they tell you to join in. You end up trying it, because you want to seem cool. And you like it! Playing the sport ends up being really fun and keeps you healthy. That wasn't a bad decision at all.

Everyone has to deal with peer pressure. You have to deal with it when you're a kid. And when you're a teen. And when you're an adult.

It's a good idea to know how to handle peer pressure now. That way, it won't be a problem when you get older. There are lots of ways to deal with peer pressure. Martial arts can teach you many things that will help you handle pressure from others.

Giving in to Peer Pressure

Why do we give in to peer pressure? Lots of reasons. Some people give in because they don't feel good about themselves. Some people give in so that other kids will like them. If everyone's doing something, even if you think it's wrong, you're more likely to do it too. Other people give in because they're afraid someone will make fun of them if they don't. It's really hard not to give in to peer pressure. But you can learn how!

2

PEER PRESSURE & MARTIAL ARTS

S tanding up to peer pressure is hard. Martial arts can help you practice handling peer pressure. Martial arts classes are safe places to practice. When you have to deal with peer pressure outside of class, you'll already know how!

Confidence

Martial arts make you feel good about yourself. When you feel good about what you can do, that's called **confidence.**

How do martial arts give you confidence? Let's say it's your very first day of class. You don't know how to do any of the moves yet. You don't know how to stand or how to do any arm blocks or kicks.

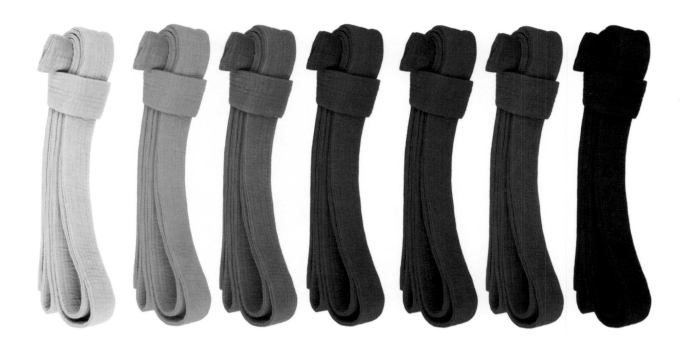

Earning a new belt can be a great way to build your confidence. It's hard work, but you'll feel good about yourself when you're putting on that new belt!

You might feel a little bad about not being able to do anything. But then you start learning. On your first day, you might learn just one or two things. But those are one or two things you didn't know how to do before!

You keep going to class. After a few weeks, you can do even more things. You feel better trying new punches and maybe even a kick.

You feel really good about everything. You've learned new things you didn't know you could do. And you feel good about trying new moves. You've learned the first ones, so why stop there?

That's confidence. You feel good about what you can do. And you're comfortable trying new things. You might not do them perfectly at first, but you'll get better. And you'll feel more confident.

A lot of the time, when we feel peer pressure, we give in. That might be because we don't feel good about ourselves. We might think the people who are pressuring us won't like us if we don't do what they say. We're not very confident of ourselves.

HANDLING PEER PRESSURE

Moving Up in Karate

Some martial arts, like karate, have levels. You know what level you're at because of the color of your belt. You start out with white. Then you move up all the way to a black belt. Moving up levels in karate helps you get self-confidence. You have to get better to move up a level. So when you move up, you feel good about yourself. You get better enough to start learning even harder things!

But if we have confidence, we can say no to peer pressure. If we don't want to do something, we can choose to not do it. We stand up for ourselves because we're confident.

Learning to Handle Peer Pressure

Martial arts are about learning how to defend yourself. But they can also teach you how to defend yourself from peer pressure.

Martial arts teachers know that kids deal with peer pressure all the time. That's why some teachers offer classes on how to handle peer pressure.

You might learn how to say no to peer pressure. You'll learn how to make your own choices. You'll learn not to let other people make you do things you don't want to do.

Handling peer pressure isn't an easy thing to learn. We aren't born knowing how to do it. We have to learn. And martial arts classes can teach you!

Good Peer Pressure

Peer pressure isn't always bad. Good peer pressure makes you do things that are good for you. Martial arts are an example of good peer pressure.

In your martial arts class, everyone is paying attention to the teacher. They're trying their best. Students are working on the moves they've learned.

You'll want to do that too, because everyone else is. Even if it's hard to focus on the teacher, you'll try. You don't want to be the only one not joining in.

You can learn martial arts at almost any age. Some students start when they're very young, but it's never too late to start learning martial arts. Make sure to practice and pay attention in class!

HANDLING PEER PRESSURE

The new moves you're trying are hard too. But lots of other people can do them. You want to too.

You might feel pressure to pay attention and try new moves. Your teacher or classmates might even tell you that you should be doing those things. Just watching other people do them is a kind of peer pressure too.

But it's good peer pressure! It will help you get better at martial arts. And you'll become a better person. Sometimes it's good to give in to peer pressure.

You just have to keep in mind which peer pressure is good. Peer pressure is good if it makes you get better at something. Maybe it's getting better at martial arts. Or getting better at paying attention in school. Or getting better at staying healthy. Peer pressure is bad when it makes you do something that could hurt you or another person.

Getting Better in Martial Arts

Martial arts help you handle peer pressure by being more confident. They also teach you how to say no to peer pressure.

Knowing how to handle peer pressure also helps you in class. If you know how to handle peer pressure, you have confidence. And that will help you get better at martial arts.

You'll feel good about trying harder things. You'll move up to the next level. And then you'll feel even better about yourself!

3

FACING PEER PRESSURE

Practicing a martial art is just one way to get better at handling peer pressure. There are other ways too. Here are some tips for dealing with peer pressure.

Think Positively!

If you don't feel good about who you are, peer pressure can be hard to handle. One of the best ways to deal with peer pressure is to feel good about yourself.

Pay attention to what you're thinking. Do you ever think bad things about yourself? Do you think, "I can't do this"? Or "I don't like the way I look"?

You might feel pressure from others to cheat on a test, but always remember what you think is right and wrong. Studying might be harder, but you'll feel better about yourself if you keep your values in mind.

Those are all **negative** thoughts. Instead, you want to think **positive** thoughts—good things about yourself.

Think about all the things you can do. Maybe you've gotten really good at martial arts. You might be able to paint really well. You may get along really well with your family. Each person has reasons to feel good about herself.

Now you just have to focus on the good things about you. Whenever you catch yourself thinking a negative thought, turn it around! Make it into something positive. If you think, "I'll never be able to play the violin," change it. Think: "I'll be able to play all these songs by the concert because I'm good at practicing every day."

When you get used to thinking good things about yourself, you'll have more confidence. So the next time someone pressures you, you can stand up to him! You can be confident about who you are and what you want to do. That makes it easier to make choices that are your own.

Know Your Values

Values are what we think is important. You might think being nice to other people is important. That's one of your values. Or you might think working hard at school is important. That's something else you value.

When you give in to peer pressure, you go against your values. If someone pressures you into being mean to someone, that might go against your value of being nice to everyone.

It helps to know what your values are. Sometimes people give in to peer pressure because they don't know what they think is important.

Let's say someone you know wants you to steal a book from your school library. You're not sure how you feel about that. On the one hand, you like reading. You have lots of books at home. It would be nice to have one more.

On the other hand, you've never stolen anything before. You think it's probably not a good thing to do. What should you decide?

If you know before you deal with peer pressure that you don't like to steal, the answer is easy. You shouldn't steal the book. But if you weren't sure how you felt about stealing, the peer pressure is harder to handle. You might say yes because you're not sure if stealing is right or wrong.

So think about what you think is wrong to do. Most people think things like cheating on tests and stealing are wrong. Come up with a list of things you don't want to do. It will be easier to say no to people who want you to do them.

Practice Saying No

When you feel peer pressure, the best thing to do is just to say no. But it's not that easy. Saying no takes practice.

Imagine someone is trying to get you to do something you don't want to do. What would you say? Remember, everything you say has to mean no.

You can start by saying why you don't want to do whatever it is you're being pressured to do. Tell your friend or the person pressuring you why you don't want to steal or skip class. Say, "I don't want to get caught." Or "I think it's wrong."

Ask the person pressuring you to do something else. If your friend is the one pressuring you, she might be okay doing something else with you. Or you can be polite and just say, "no thanks." Then try to change the subject.

Whenever you're saying no, stand up straight. Look the person in the eye if you can. Show the person pressuring you that you're confident. He'll be more likely to just leave you alone.

And be sure to leave the area as soon as you can if you need to. If you're on the playground, go to a different part. If you're walking home from school, walk quickly so you get home faster.

Talk to Someone

We all deal with peer pressure sometimes. So it's good to talk to other people about it. Talk to your friends. Ask them if they've ever had to deal with peer pressure. What did they do about it?

You can also talk to your family. Your parents might have some good advice. Brothers, sisters, and cousins might too. They'll be able to make you feel better about being peer pressured. They'll let you know that you aren't alone in feeling peer pressure.

Talking to adults can help in other ways too. Your teacher, school guidance counselor, or another adult can help make peer pressure stop. If someone is peer pressuring you to do something you don't want to, it's not okay. You can tell an adult.

Those adults might have good ways to stop the peer pressure. They can tell you how to handle it yourself. Or they can talk to the person pressuring you. They can do something about it. If you sit next to someone who is pressuring you in class, for example, your teacher can move your seats around.

Pick Good Friends

Good friends don't pressure you. They don't force you to do things you don't want to do. People who pressure you aren't your friends.

Try to find friends who think the same things are important as you do. That way, they won't peer pressure you to do things you think are wrong.

For example, you think it's important that you do all your homework. You wouldn't want to cheat and copy someone else's homework. But you have a friend who always wants to copy off your work. You don't like it, but you let her because you think she's your friend.

A really good friend wouldn't copy from you. She would see it makes you feel bad. So she wouldn't pressure you into letting her copy your homework.

If you are feeling a lot of peer pressure to do things you don't want to do, the best thing to do may be to look for different people to hang out with. Are there other kids in your class that think doing homework is important? You can probably find lots of people who wouldn't ask you to let them copy your homework. Maybe you could even do your homework together, and help each other.

If you start hanging out with those friends, you won't feel peer pressure. No one will be asking you to do something you don't want to do. And you'll have some great new friends!

Taekwondo and Peer Pressure

At some taekwondo schools, teachers have their students practice handling peer pressure. During class, everyone takes a break from practicing strikes and kicks. The teacher picks a volunteer and pretends to be a kid pressuring the volunteer. The volunteer has to practice saying no to the peer pressure. He might ask the teacher, "Why are you pressuring me?" Or say, "Stop pressuring me." Everyone else in class can help the volunteer. It's a safe place to practice handling peer pressure. No one will actually make a student do anything. Practice makes perfect!

4

PEER PRESSURE & YOUR LIFE

K nowing how to handle peer pressure can help you every day. Peer pressure is a part of normal life. That's why we need to know how to handle it!

How Do You Feel?

When you give in to peer pressure, you might feel bad. You could be sad. Or worried if you're doing something you know you shouldn't be.

You might feel guilty. Or **disappointed** in yourself. If you know better than to steal, but you do it anyway, you'll feel like you let yourself down.

It's normal to feel bad sometimes. But you shouldn't make yourself feel bad! You need to learn how to say no to peer pressure so you don't end up feeling bad.

When you know how to handle peer pressure, you feel good. You'll be proud of yourself for saying no to things you don't want to do. You'll be happy. You'll feel confident that you can stand up for yourself. That's a lot better than feeling bad all the time!

Making Real Friends

We all want friends who are fun to hang out with and good to talk to. You probably want friends who like doing the same things you do. You want friends who make you feel happy. When you know how to handle peer pressure, you'll end up with these kinds of friends.

Sometimes people you think are friends pressure you into doing things you don't want to do. But you don't want to hang out with those people. So you look for friends who don't pressure you. And you'll find that you really like those people! You can do things together that are comfortable for all of you.

School

School is where a lot of peer pressure happens. If you're always afraid of being pressured, school can be really hard.

Peer pressure will probably happen to you at school no matter what. But if you know how to handle it, it's not a big deal.

You can make school less scary by learning about peer pressure. Once you know what it is and how to handle it, it doesn't have to ruin your day.

Whether it's on the playground or in class, you'll be prepared. You'll be confident in yourself. And you know how to say no. If peer pressure happens to you, it just won't be a big deal!

Peer pressure can be scary, but it doesn't have to be! Martial arts help you learn how to handle peer pressure. So next time you have to deal with peer

Good friends won't push you to do something you don't want to. They want you to feel good about yourself because they care. Good friends won't pressure you.

pressure, calm down. Say no. Think about how confident you are. Remember what you learned in class.

Martial artists are prepared for all sorts of things. They can defend themselves. They can do fancy kicks and punches. But they can also fight peer pressure. It's one of the most important things you can learn while you practice martial arts!

Good Peer Pressure

Here are some more things that are good peer pressure. If everyone is doing these things, you should make up your mind to do them too!

Be nice to others
Work hard at school
Exercise and do sports
Stay away from drugs and alcohol
Be respectful

Words to Know:

compete: To go against at least one other person in a sport or activity to see who wins.

confidence: Feeling good about who you are and what you can do.

disappointed: Feeling let down when you expected something to be good.

flexible: Able to bend or stretch the body.

negative: Having to do with something that makes you feel bad about yourself.

positive: Having to do with something that makes you feel good.

practiced: Learned, used, and trained to become better at something.

self-defense: Stopping another person from hurting you and making sure you're safe from danger.

skills: Things you learn that help you become a better person or live a better life.

Find Out More

Online

Kids Health: Peer Pressure
kidshealth.org/kid/feeling/emotion/peer_pressure.html

KidzWorld: Martial Arts Quiz
www.kidzworld.com/quiz/5917-quiz-martial-arts-trivia

Martial Arts History Museum
martialartsmuseum.com

In Books

Cooper, Scott. *Speak Up and Get Along!* Minneapolis, Minn.: Free Spirit Publishing, 2005.

Scandiffio, Laura. *The Martial Arts Book*. Toronto, Ont.: Annick Press, 2010.

Wiseman, Blaine. *Martial Arts*. New York: AV2 Books, 2010.

Index

About the Author

Kim Etingoff lives in Boston, Massachusetts, spending part of her time working on farms. Kim writes educational books for young people on topics including health, nutrition, and more.

Picture Credits: